George Washington

A Biography of an American President

Table of Contents

Introduction

"Associate yourself with men of good quality, if you esteem your own reputation; for 'tis better to be alone than in bad company." — George Washington

There is quite a bit of pedigree that comes with being the first in any role or position. Most specifically, you get to set the tone and expectations for those who come after you. As there is no expectation or previous failures for you to repeat, there is less pressure to uphold the reputation of someone who had held the position before you. Moreover, as there was no one preceding you, any accomplishments you make will be the first of their own kind, again setting the stage of expectation for all those that follow and take over after you.

Unfortunately, there is also a great deal of pressure that comes with being the first. When you are first there is no one there to come before you, to help guide you in the right direction or advise you when you are perhaps leading astray. Adding to this pressure is the fact that many individuals who are first in their position have, quite literally, a plethora of individuals who are following their lead and guidance, all of whom the person is responsible for, in one way or another. Thus, being the first in a position culminates in a contradictory state of being. You must simultaneously guide those under you through whatever path or journey your position dictates, while at the same time forging your own path. You must present yourself, to those below you, as a confident leader who is knowledgeable about the road ahead, while at the same time developing your own knowledge about the unknown future. All of this is to say that being the first, in any position, is not an easy job that should be taken lightly.

One of the most prestigious firsts is the focus of this book. Through the following chapters you will get a comprehensive look into the life, career, and death of the first president of the United States: George Washington. Beginning with the childhood of this great man, you will be brought on a journey that includes Washington's political and military life before claiming the title of president. Following this, you will be brought through the Washington presidency, and ending with his life beyond politics and the legacy he has left behind. Interspaced between the chapters you will find some memorable and lasting quotes once uttered by this great man that many still consider to be important today.

No matter your previous knowledge of Mr. Washington, upon reading this book, you will have a well-rounded understanding of who the first president of The United States was, the pressures it took for him to lead one of the most powerful countries in the world, and the incredible lessons that have lasted for centuries following his death.

Without further ado let us begin your introduction to, arguably, one of the most powerful men in the history of the United States: Mr. George Washington.

* * *

"Real men despise battle, but will never run from it."
— *George Washington*

Chapter One: Young George Washington

"My mother was the most beautiful woman I ever saw. All I am I owe to my mother. I attribute my success in life to the moral, intellectual and physical education I received from her." — George Washington

On the 22nd of February in 1732, Mary Bell Washington gave birth to her first son with her husband Augustine Washington on a farm in Westmoreland County, Virginia. Little did she and her husband know that this new-born boy would become a founding father and first sitting president of the United States of America.

Mary was the second wife of Augustine, who had not only been married before, but had two sons from his previous marriage: Lawrence and Augustine. Therein making Mary's firstborn child technically the third in their family. After George, Mary and Augustine had five other children: three more boys and two girls. George and his family, while always living on a farm or plantation of sorts, moved around quite often during his childhood. This consistent moving was due to his father's ownership of multiple different plots of land.

As a child, George was noticeably talented and excelled in many areas. He grew to be a very tall and strong young boy, who was generally and overall quite physically talented; he is noted in many history books as being the fastest and strongest of his brothers and friends. As such, and perhaps due to his great natural physical ability, he became quite a talented and skilled horseman, able to ride and control nearly every horse he was put on, through any sort of terrain and path.

In addition to his physical prowess, Washington showed great promise with his academics, even from a young age. He excelled in almost every subject while being home-schooled by his mother, so much so, in fact, that Washington's mother and father had plans for him to be sent overseas to England to finish his education. Unfortunately, this plan of finishing his higher-level education overseas came to halt when he was eleven years old, as tragedy struck George and his family.

In 1743, Augustine Washington, George's father, passed away suddenly, leaving Mary alone with the seven children. Thankfully the family had been well off and prosperous for the majority of their lives, so the loss of their father did not leave them financially strained. George's father's estate, inheritance, and legacy were divided evenly among all of the children and George's mother; with the two older and half-brothers receiving their own share and the rest going to Mary to be divided evenly amongst the rest of their children.

With the head of the family gone, George stepped up in his role as one of the eldest children and helped his mother raise his younger siblings. However, this meant that George was left without a father figure or guidance in his teenage and young adult years. When it came time to finish his education, George attended different schools within the American colonies and even moved in with his older half-brother Lawrence to ensure his studies came first. Lawrence, as a result, became a second father to George in a pivotal time in his life.

While George's family was generally well-off and made their work on their different plantation sites the priority of their day-to-day lives, they were also deeply religious. Posthumously, there have been many accounts detailing Washington's reading of the bible, keeping a religious and faith-based set of values throughout his life. These values were instilled in the young George Washington, in addition to the importance of hard and efficient work.

One notable aspect of George's childhood and young life is that his family, being wealthy, owned many slaves over several of their plantations. In fact, when George's father passed in the mid 1700s, part of his inheritance that was passed on to the rest of his family were slaves, each member receiving some. Specifically, it has been noted somewhere that between 9-12 slaves were passed on to George. While the specific number remains to be clarified, many believe that the exact number was

10, but some reports differ. It is interesting to consider that an eleven-year-old, as part of an inheritance from his father, received people. Historians then note that this installment of the normalcy of owning and trading slaves was what led to George owning, controlling, and trading over 500 slaves in his lifetime.

While he ended up owning his own line and group of plantations that ranged the American colonies, George spent the majority of his life living at a small hunting plantation now known internationally as Mount Vernon. It is here where he brought his wife, Martha (née Dandridge Custis) in 1759, and where they established their own family and set of numerous slaves, some of which would be passed down and inherited by his own children.

Stories From Washington's Childhood

Many historians attribute the childhood of George Washington to the kind of man and leader he eventually became. As with many individuals once they become nationally known, once hitting these positions of influence, storytellers and biographers flesh through the stories and events of their childhood to see if any specific experience or event was a key point of influence in creating who they became. For George Washington, this trend is ever-present.

In this search for stories and events from his past, there have been two events and experiences in George's childhood that many consider to be key moments and instances where he showed the kind of honorable and honest man he would one day become.

Washington and The Colt

The first story is said to not only show the bravery and courage that allowed Washington to lead armies through battle and, eventually, the population of a newly formed independent nation. But this childhood tale also shows the honesty, humility, and empathy he had which made him a relatable person of leadership. The story is as follows:

Out of the many horses that resided on the many different plantations his family owned, there was one that was unruly and had proven, time and time again, to be untamable. Many slaves, horse riders, and relatives of the Washington's had tried to ride the colt, but all had failed. In fact, so many had failed that it was understood amongst all who came across this colt that he was untamable and unrideable. After several years of trying, no one ever managed to mount and ride the colt.

Even with the untamable characteristic and personality, this colt was Mary, George's mother's, favorite horse. She would repeatedly praise the horse for being wild and untamable. She fearfully respected the horse for its nature and came to love the horse as her own, even though she could not ride him. She therefore made the slaves, other employees, and people on the plantation treat it with care and respect.

While most listened to her wishes, and stayed away from trying to mount the colt, George saw the instability of the colt as a challenge. One afternoon, George gathered his brothers, many of his friends, and some slaves to try and close in on the colt. Eventually, and after much effort, the group was able to corner the colt and put a harness on its back. Without even questioning his ability, George jumped on the back of the colt.

The colt tried with all of his might to kick and flip his rider off of him; however, it was without luck. George stayed strong in his position and kept atop the great animal. Unfortunately, in the exertion of trying to force George off of his back, the colt busted a blood vessel and ended up collapsing on the ground dead. Shocked by the events, all involved participants fled the scene.

However that night, when Mary found the deceased colt, she questioned her sons, and slaves as to what had happened. While the rest of those involved stayed quiet out of fear of being reprimanded, George spoke up telling his mother the truth. He took responsibility for the event, as it was he who had ridden the colt to its unfortunate death.

According to those present, George's mother, while incredibly saddened by the death of her most favorite horse, was overcome with joy and pride that her son had the courage and honesty to not only tell her the truth of what happened but to take responsibility for his actions. She was so proud that she forgave him instantly for the incident and never brought it up again, unless it was to praise her son for his behavior.

Washington and The Cherry Tree

The story of George Washington and the cherry tree is probably one of the most popular and well-known stories of this president's childhood. It was recorded in many history books as being a critical and pivotal moment that showed the strength and determination of the young man, in addition to being courageous in his honesty and leadership. It should be noted however that unfortunately, over time, this story was deemed to likely be false as it was most likely made up by a biographer and Washington historian, Mason Locke Weems. That being said, it still stands to be one of the most popular stories of George Washington's childhood and is still considered a tale that exemplifies the qualities valued in him as a president that were seen as a young man.

The story is as follows:

When George Washington was a young man, around the age of nine or ten, he became the owner and master of a hatchet. Overjoyed by this gift, Washington spent many days practicing how to use the hatchet in order to yield it with great power and efficiency. Washington considered this hatchet to be one of the most powerful of its kind. Once he considered himself an expert in controlling the power of the hatchet, he spent many of his days showing individuals how strong this hatchet actually was. He would do so by exploring through the gardens and all around his family plantations, cutting down anything in his path. While every once in a while he would find a plant or object that would challenge the strength of the hatchet, he never once gave into the strength of the object he was cutting, and was always able to conquer the plant with the power and sharpness of his tool.

One day, however, George found himself face-to-face with a cherry tree. This cherry tree, then staring George down as if to challenge him, was the favorite and most prized possession of his father. No one was to ever harm or even touch the cherry tree without Washington's father's approval and permission. While a modest cherry tree, it stood tall and strong, yielding many years' worth of stone fruit. On this day, however, the reputation of this prized cherry tree presented itself more as a challenge to the young George Washington.

Perhaps accidentally, or perhaps out of curiosity, George swung his ax and was shocked at how easily the hatchet penetrated the trunk of the cherry tree. Simultaneously George was impressed at the resistance and strength the cherry tree reciprocated as it still stood tall over him. Of course, with a few more swings of his powerful hatchet, George was able to conquer his challenger and bring it to the ground. Once the battle was completed, George realized what he had done and ran back to his home swearing to hide the truth from anyone who asked.

However, that night when George's father asked his family what had happened to one of his prized possessions, the young president-to-be could not resist the urge to divulge the truth. He stood in front of his father and told him the adventure he had had that day with his hatchet and his confrontation with the cherry tree. Again, and in similar fashion to his mother with the colt, George's father, although sad at the loss of his cherry tree, was incredibly and boastfully proud of his son for telling the truth. As the story goes, George's father exclaimed with great joy the courage and honesty his young son had and how he was destined for great things, due to these character traits that he had exhibited on this day.

As you can see these two stories, whether truthful or not, both exemplify and show the theory that George Washington was a courageous leader who valued honesty and never backed away from a challenge from a very young age. Generally, among many scholars and historians, George Washington's childhood, and privilege therein, allowed for him to grow up well educated in the areas of law, philosophy, governance, and world history. He was overall said to be a well-rounded, polite, hardworking, and honest young man. Traits that would undoubtedly follow him throughout the rest of his life and lead to his monumental success in politics.

* * *

"It is better to offer no excuse than a bad one."
—*George Washington*

Chapter Two: Early Political and Military Career

"99% of failures come from people who make excuses." —
George Washington

Political Life

George Washington first stepped into the political arena in 1758 when he was elected to the House of Burgesses, the legislative body of the Colony of Virginia. Specifically, he was named the representative of Frederick County. At this time the thirteen colonies, each having their own governor and small number of representatives, were largely governed on their own, yet were still being controlled and dictated by the King of England at the time: King George III.

For the first decade or so, as part of the Virginia government, George Washington played a small part as a lower-level official and public servant, working on those causes that were close to his heart and interest. Fortunately, by being a lower-level public servant within his colony's government, Washington was able to maintain his role and profession of farmer and plantation owner.

That being said, this does not mean that Washington did not have a hand in some of the larger and more influential political issues during the mid-to-late 1700s; most of them leading to or having some sort of relation to the mounting conflict with the British laws under which the American Colonies were limited and ruled by.

After his experiences with certain, arguably smaller military roles and battles—that is smaller in comparison to the larger group of battles under the heading of the Revolutionary war—Washington became a louder political voice within the Colonies of America. The manner in which he conducted his politics was what largely stood out to other members of both Virginia and to the Colonies as a whole. For example, after supporting and pushing for a friend's candidacy into the Virginia House of Burgess, conflict erupted with other members and candidates, specifically with another Virginian named William Payne. While tension increased between Washington and Payne, many, including Payne, believed that a duel was to happen; however, Washington approached his adversary and apologized for the tension and conflict. This was an act of conflict resolution that did not go unnoticed by the other political members of his states. This would help to set up his future as the political leader of a country.

While many individuals, both established political figures and scholars alike, from other colonies as well as his own, were pushing for the revolution and independence from England, Washington in his early years was never in total agreement with these radical thinkers. In fact, Washington opposed the idea of total independence from England for many years, even while being a member of government. Rather, what Washington pushed and worked for as his political agenda was fairness between England and the American colonies.

However, in 1770 Washington's political views and agendas changed slightly and became more radical. As a farmer, both in familial tradition and in his present-day life, Washington experienced and understood the difficulties of that profession. Specifically, the frustration of receiving less money for his products that he was shipping over to England, in addition to the high cost and prices of the items that were bought from and traded with England. What added to this frustration was the fact that selling items back to England was a necessary part of the agreement between England and the colonies. This unfairness of trade is said to be what drove Washington to officially join the revolutionary movement.

To put it simply, as things got worse, he became more vocal towards the revolutionary cause and the fairness of farmers and plantation owners in the American Colonies. It should be noted that while Washington never fully endorsed the idea of war; he thought the idea of violence to obtain a desired outcome was unnecessary. In fact, he only considered war as a final resort when the person, or groups of persons, working against you become hostile themselves. Eventually, as the mounting conflict turned violent, Washington saw that he could do nothing but agree with and join the fight.

It was this joining of the Revolutionary movement, paired with his military prowess and experience, that made him a formidable choice to lead the armies and revolutionary cause to its victory.

Military Life

The military life of George Washington, especially his early military life, is an interesting one. This is due in part to the fact that Washington was never necessarily considered a violent or aggressive child. Nor was he ever deemed a person who enjoyed conquering others, even for the purposes of fairness, equality, and independence.

That being said, the entrance of George Washington into the military was perhaps a no-brainer based on his family's history. His two older, and half-brothers, Augustine and Lawrence, had both made significant influence and were seen as important members of their respective armies in their respective and specific battles. Many Washington scholars and historians attribute Washington's shift and interest in the military to the fact that he was raised by these two older brothers for the majority of his life. For instance, his half-brother Lawrence, the brother who essentially acted as Washington's father after their father had passed years earlier, had served as an adjutant general of the Virginia militia; generally, he developed into the role of general that many lieutenant governors relied on.

However, when Lawrence died of tuberculosis in the early 1750s, Lieutenant Governor Robert Dinwiddie, turned to Lawrence's half-brother George for aid and replacement. This happened of course due to how close George and Lawrence were and how much Lawrence influenced George in warlike conflict. In fact, it was Dinwiddie that gave Washington his first employment within a war. Specifically, he sent George Washington to the French posts to warn them to stop their assault on the Ohio Valley. Eventually, the warning was one of violent threats, saying that if they did not see to the end their movement, then they would have to deal with more severe hardship and war to come. The task to deliver such a note of threats was a hard and futile journey as the French Commander, although cordial to Washington and his fellow comrades, was hard-headed in his position to abide by the request of Dinwiddie and abandon his assault. The task proved increasingly difficult as on his return to the base camp to report what had transpired, he was shot at multiple times, and almost died due to the freezing weather and hypothermia in the Allegheny River. This of course, was in addition to the fact that the journey itself took over 70 days, an aspect of the journey that was not necessarily enjoyable to begin with. However, it was due to his fulfillment of the task, even if the French Commander did not respond ideally to the message, that led Governor Robert Dinwiddie to repeatedly use Washington in several posts in upcoming wars.

It was this repetition of use by Dinwiddie that gave Washington the confidence and pedigree he needed to officially be entered into the military, a move that happened in 1753. Washington became himself a natural, powerful, and intelligent leader who played an integral part of whatever battle he was a part of.

During the French and Indian War, Dinwiddie promoted George Washington to the title of lieutenant colonel, and gave Washington leadership abilities over a three hundred men regiment in Virginia. Following different orders to defeat the French forces, Washington proved himself to be an integral part of fighting the French and Indian War. Many times, he refused payment or title when given additional responsibilities throughout the war. As such, Washington notably said that he would choose to volunteer his services many times rather than be paid to do so.

Over his years as a low-level soldier, being given high levels of responsibility, Washington noticed that there was a high amount of disorganization, a sense of destructive competition, and a general lack of consensus of intention among the different lieutenant generals, under which he served. As a result,

Washington developed strong support for the need for a centralized Government system that unified the colonies. Little did he know that he would, in fact, be acting as the individual to take up this first unifying position.

The Revolutionary War

In June of 1975, George Washington was nominated to be commander and chief of the Continental Army during the Revolutionary War. Washington was chosen over others such as John Hancock on account of his previous military experience. It was due to his past successes and experiences in the military that it was believed that Washington, by being able to keep his own ambition and intentions in check, would be able to keep an army poised for revolution in check as well. However, it is also said that Washington was chosen due to Virginia's power and influence over the other colonies. It was believed that only an individual from Virginia would be influential enough to unite all of the colonies against the British Monarchy. After a week of only slight deliberation, Washington was named general and commander-in-chief of the army of the United Colonies.

His first move as commander in chief was of course to choose and build a shortlist of primary staff and officers to help him during the war against the British. Among these individuals are many notable names, including Major General Charles Lee,

Major General Philip Schuyler, Colonel Henry Knox, and Colonel Alexander Hamilton. Generally speaking, Washington poised and presented himself as being a rather sensible revolutionary and military leader. However, it was noted by many who followed his rule that, for the first phase of the Revolutionary War, Washington always seemed to be fighting the war on the defensive. That is to say, while Washington never truly gave up too much ground in the war and was seen to be fighting the war successfully, it was suggested that he was always reacting to what the British were doing rather than being proactive and making headway in the war.

In fact, Washington failed in many smaller instances during the Revolutionary War and chose to be too trusting of some of his staff officers and subordinates. As some historians may recount, Washington put his trust into certain individuals who had yet to show their prowess in the line of duty.

No matter when the official turning point was, what is important to note is that in the midst of his failures, in addition to his successes, Washington remained the same sort of leader throughout the entirety of the Revolutionary War. He was fiercely protective of his officers and army men who gave him their loyalty and lives in the name of American freedom. Washington created a sense of confidence, and was seen as one who can be trusted with the lives of thousands of men at one time, and one that could lead the American colonies to victory.

This image of a competent leader, even considering his many failures in battle, was deeply rooted in the fact that Washington created a type of national spirit surrounding the revolution. Therefore, while some of the army men and officers did not wholeheartedly agree with Washington as a leader, they related to and fully supported his intention and goal for the war. Furthermore, while some of his army men did not necessarily consider him to be an exemplary military leader, they did consider him to be an exemplary leader of moral standing and of mankind, which in turn led them to consistently follow him into different battles throughout the Revolutionary War.

For example, Washington made it quite clear that he had no time for anyone who was cowardly, inefficient, dishonest, or disloyal to either himself, the country they were trying to create, or the mere intention and idea of freedom from the monarchy. Washington allowed for failure among the men, but he did not allow for cowardice, immorality, or selfishness.

Part of his leadership abilities was that Washington understood that each and every battle has a winner and a loser based on strategy, number of men, and a wide variety of additional factors. For this reason, he did not reprimand any of his army men if a battle was a failure. He deemed the many losses of life, which were sacrificed during battle, as failure enough. It was indeed any man who was dishonest, immoral, or not enthusiastic towards the idea of freedom from the monarchy that was the true insult and failure in the eyes of George Washington. In fact, through correspondence and diaries kept of the men during the Revolutionary War, it was well known that Washington would flog or otherwise reprimand men who showed unappreciative personal qualities as a way of using them as an example for others.

This distinction and balancing act between being seen as a less than successful military General, yet a highly regarded and respected leader, followed Washington from the Revolutionary War and into his two terms as president of the United States.

Politics

It is perhaps interesting to note that the first president of the United States was reluctant to both enter into the world of politics and enter into the world of military combatants: two areas of which the president of the United States necessarily must, or at least is highly encouraged to, have some experience in. His entrance into both the political and military realms were not an accident, and although being reluctant to do so Washington entered both arenas willingly and with great force.

One trend that is noticeable through the life of George Washington, with specific reference to his early political and military experiences, was that he entered into both arenas out of a sense of duty; duty for a country that had yet to be established.

To reiterate or summarize, he entered into politics as his life and livelihood as a farmer and plantation owner was beginning to be negatively affected by the laws set in place by the British monarchy. Moreover, he entered into the military out of his sense of duty and respect to avenge the life of his half-brother Lawrence. In both the case of his early political career and his early military career, George Washington began as a low-level associate and moved up the ranks, increasingly being given more and more responsibility as he showed that his leadership qualities were far beyond those exhibited by anyone else.

From the revolutionary battles of the Siege of Boston to the Valley Forge and finally, to the success and victory at Yorktown, George Washington proved that he could lead the colonies through the bloodshed of the Revolutionary War by creating a sense of unified patriotism that encouraged men across the American Colonies to take up arms against the oppressive British rule. This skill set would prove beneficial again when the colonies were tasked with coming together as one, to form a newly freed and established country.

* * *

"Human happiness and moral duty are inseparably connected." —George Washington

Chapter Three: The First President of the United States

"A free people ought not only to be armed, but disciplined; to which end a uniform and well-digested plan is requisite; and their safety and interest require that they should promote such manufactories as tend to render them independent of others for essential, particularly military, supplies." —George Washington

George Washington's Presidency in Summary

On the 30th of April 1789, George Washington swore his oath to become the first president of the United States, in what was then the capital of this newly formed country, New York City. As John Adams had received the second most number of votes in the election he was named the vice president. While George Washington was overwhelmingly chosen as president, it should be noted that, at that time, there were still a few states that had not yet ratified the Constitution to be part of this newly formed country and were therefore unable to vote. Washington was overwhelmingly and unanimously chosen as president, largely thanks to the method and system of voting that was in place during this first presidential election. Specifically, every electorate was able to vote twice. This two-voting system allowed the electorate to vote however they wanted twice, without the requirement of placing both votes on one candidate. It was recorded that every electorate who voted in this first presidential election used at least one of their votes on choosing Washington as president. It was therefore considered that Washington was voted into the presidential role unanimously, as technically, every electorate voted for him. The same thing happened in Washington's second presidential election: every person used at least one of their votes on George Washington becoming president.

It should also be noted that, interestingly, at the end of repeating his sworn oath Washington added the phrase "so help me God." What was merely meant to be a phrase he uttered out of sheer honesty and admission, was deemed impressive and was then added to sworn oaths of accepting the presidency. In other words, what was meant to be a mutter to himself is now used in every presidential sworn oath.

One of the first actions Washington took once admitted to office, was that he assembled his cabinet; that is, he assembled a group of men whom he respected to assist him in running the country. These members of his cabinet are no strangers to our history books. The secretary of state was Thomas Jefferson, the Secretary of War was Henry Knox, the Secretary of Treasury was Alexander Hamilton, and the Chief Justice was John Jay. All of whom had integral and strongly influential roles in the Revolutionary War that led to the independence of the United States and to Washington becoming president. There were a few other notable members of Washington's Council that, although were not official members of his cabinet, were deemed high-level advisors; perhaps most notably of these men was James Madison.

Another notable aspect of the Washington presidency as a whole, is that he was sure to make it clear that he did not want to be called "Your Highness" by the people of the United States. As he had spent his entire life under the reign of a king, he thought that making the population of the United States call him your highness was slightly hypocritical, as they just forced their independence from a monarchy. Rather he asked that they call him Mister President; a title that has lasted from the formation of the United States to the present day.

There are a few different theories as to why he asked to be called such a title. However, perhaps one of the most entertaining notions is that everything he did during this role set the stage and expectation for those leaders in the coming years. As such, since he was setting so many precedents, he chose to be called Mister President.

After only his first term, and first four years of being president, George Washington wanted to retire, as his home life was calling to him to come back. However, he was asked to serve again. After much deliberation, he accepted the role of president for another term. When these four years had expired, he was asked once more to serve as president. However, this time he refused. His refusal is based largely on a few stringent reasons. The first of course being that he was hesitant to accept the presidency in the first place, as he felt his heart was back home on his plantations and farms with his family. The second reason was that he wanted to set the precedent of the United States being different from the country from which they just emancipated themselves. While England had one ruler until that ruler passed away or was overthrown, the United States should have a type of replacement strategy for their leaders. The fact that Washington voluntarily stepped down after only two terms set the stage for every president to follow: to only be allowed two terms within the position. At least this was true until Franklin Delano Roosevelt took office who in fact served for four terms; however, that was nearly one hundred and fifty years into the future.

Essentially, a simple summary of Washington's presidency is that it was a presidency of precedents. Every notion Washington passed, every move Washington made, and every decision Washington made, was the first of its kind and would set the stage for a variety of presidential reigns to follow.

His First Term

The majority of his first term as president was largely based around the organization of a new government for a newly formed nation. George Washington set up and organized new administrative procedures, military actions, and financial systems, in addition to a variety of different presidential and governmental traditions that formed what the United States was as a country.

In his first inaugural address, Washington admitted that he was unpracticed in the ways of governing, yet he would do his best to maintain fairness and integrity in his position to ensure that the repercussions of war and the emancipation from England were well worth it for their new nation. On account of this unpracticed and perhaps naivete in the position, Washington relied on many of his advisors for help to develop certain areas of the country. For example, stemming from their close relationship during the Revolutionary War, Washington leaned heavily on Hamilton for financial advice and guidance in the new financial system of the government.

However, while Washington relied heavily on those around him, he was still deemed a successful president as he set the ideal expectation of what a president should be. That is a man who is humble and honest, yet confident in his own abilities and of the expertise of those with whom he surrounds himself. Washington's honesty, fairness, and integrity in the position of president were what many presidents that followed him aspired to be.

Of course, this first term of the Washington presidency was not all organizational, nor was Washington's decision to lean on his cabinet members approved by everyone. This was because many of his cabinet members did not necessarily get along with each other and in fact quite publicly refuted each other's beliefs and political agendas. Perhaps most notably, was Madison's and Jefferson's distaste for the Secretary of Treasury Alexander Hamilton. This distaste between cabinet members however did not remain solely within the cabinet. Rather, it began to spread throughout what would grow to be a multi-party political system within the United States. This made the first term of the Washington presidency not only one where the new president leaned on his cabinet members, but one where the new president had to balance and play peacekeeper between certain members of his cabinet, in addition to running the nation!

His Second Term

Setting itself apart from his first term, the second term of George Washington's presidency was largely focused on foreign affairs. The French Revolution was gaining speed in Europe. This world event led to the big question of whether or not the United States was meant to help the French in their goal for independence. Due to the fact that the United States was still recovering from their own independence and Revolutionary War, Washington opted to not send military or financial aid to the French in their own revolution.

While this decision was hotly debated and largely disagreed with by members of the United States government and George Washington's cabinet, Washington stood firm in his decision. His reasoning for such a decision was that it would allow the United States to become more financially independent, and more stable as a nation unto itself. Washington feared that if he would join in the revolution with the French, he would not only lose large amounts of the United States population, but he would lengthen the healing and reparation time from their own revolution.

While Washington, during his second term, seemingly became more comfortable in his role, he still largely leaned on and was influenced by the opinions of his cabinet members. As such he unintentionally caused the separation and creation of a multi-party political system.

That being said, there were other significant events during his second term. Perhaps most notably, was that the long-lasting Indian war in the northwest of the American colonies had ended. Spain released their hold on their territory and the northwest was available and open for settlement of the American people.

Essentially, the second term of the president gave him the confidence to make more drastic decisions about the United States relationship with the rest of the world, in addition to giving the newly formed country a longer time to repair and steady itself. It should also be noted, that while many disagreed with Washington's treatment and handling of the French Revolution during his second term, he was still asked enthusiastically to return for a third term as president. However, this time Washington refused and stuck to his decision to do so, consequently, leading to the Adams Administration taking over the role.

* * *

"However [political parties] may now and then answer popular ends, they are likely in the course of time and things, to become potent engines, by which cunning, ambitious, and unprincipled men will be enabled to subvert the power of the people and to usurp for themselves the reins of government, destroying afterwards the very engines which have lifted them to unjust dominion." — *George Washington*

Chapter Four: Memorable Moments of His Presidency

"A primary object should be the education of our youth in the science of government. In a republic, what species of knowledge can be equally important? And what duty is more pressing than communicating it to those who are to be the future guardians of the liberties of the country?" —George Washington

Arguably the largest and most monumental moment of George Washington's terms as president was that he was in fact the first of a long line of presidents. He set the tone for many who have come after him, for what should and should not be done in such a role. Besides the importance of his initial firstness in the position, there are many other moments that must be taken note of and remembered as being unique to his run in the position.

For example, let us take into account and examine the statutes and precedents that he set, almost accidentally, that have lasted well over two hundred years. To mention a few by name, his candid and improvisational adage to the oath is now taken by every new president that is sworn into the position. Other examples of memorable accidents that have been turned into presidential traditions—some of which have actually been written into the Constitution of the United States—ranging from Washington asking to be called "president" rather than something relating to monarchy, to the length of time all future presidents will be able to take up the role and position.

Aside from these perhaps accidental or coincidental standards that Washington set during his presidency, there are arguably two moments, or two collections of moments, rather, that stand apart from all others. The first is his participation in the ratification and actual creation of the Bill of Rights and the Constitution of the United States; that is, his participation in the actual forming of the United States rather than simply fighting for its freedom. The second collection of moments was Washington's manner in which he left the White House and role of the presidency.

Contributions to The Constitution

Beginning on May 14th, 1787, fifty-five representatives and delegates from 12 of the 13 states arrived in Philadelphia Pennsylvania to revise the Articles of the Confederation, under the new lens that the United States was now its own country, free from the rule of the British Monarchy. It should be noted that Rhode Island did not send any delegates or representatives from their state to the Constitutional Convention; the exact reason has not yet been confirmed by historians.

Out of these 55 representatives there are some rather historically notable names including Alexander Hamilton, Benjamin Franklin, James Madison, and John Mercer—Mercer being the eventual grandfather of Lucy Mercer the woman with whom Franklin Delano Roosevelt had a torrid affair.

Although the intention of the constitutional convention was simply to revise and update the Articles of the Confederation together, the four-month-long debate turned into something that proved to be much more historically significant; mainly the creation of the Constitution of the United States.

As chaos and disagreements began to erupt at the beginning stages of the convention, many of the delegates agreed that there needed to be a head or president of the convention in order to preside over the group as a whole; to encourage a streamlined and less confrontational atmosphere. Unanimously, George Washington was voted for this position, as it was well known to his compatriots of his leadership qualities throughout the Revolutionary War and the victory over the British.

Within the 4 months to follow, the Federalists and the Anti-Federalists would debate, argue, and hotly discuss what the statutes of their newly formed country should be. This gave the delegates and representatives their first taste of how difficult establishing and running a new free country can be.

However, it has been noted that George Washington did in fact ease the process of the creation of the Constitution. It was found through the correspondence of many who attended the Constitutional Convention to those who had not attended, that it was Washington who allowed for and encouraged an environment of compromise and understanding between the over 50 independent voices that were shouting their own state plan of how the government of the United States should run.

In the end, on September 17th, 1787, Washington guided the Constitutional Convention to a seven-article document, in addition to a preamble and closing statement of endorsement. This original Constitution embodied a democratic compromise between the states that would set up the United States as being a truly democratic country free from the monarchy. It would allow the United States to what it desired to be: a country that wants to do its best for the individuals that reside within it.

Admittedly, the original Constitution of the United States was not complete in its creation. This is because many of the ideas that were presented were negotiated against and ultimately left out of the original Constitution out of fear that implementing too much governmental power or change would be rejected by the people of the United States. For this reason, these delegates and members of the convention left out laws and rights that they believed would eventually be written into the Constitution over time. Of course, they were correct in this assumption. Since its first instantiation, the Constitution of the United States has been amended 27 times. The first ten of these amendments are often referred to as the Bill of Rights. The majority of these over 20 total amendments and adjustments to the Constitution, largely had to do with the Civil Rights of the population, as the rights of both women and black individuals were eventually acknowledged.

While there have been many arguments against the original Constitution, in addition to the fact that the Constitution has been amended and ratified many times over since its creation, Washington played a pivotal role in allowing for both the establishment of the United States as a country and for the developments that have been made in the years to follow. This is because it was Washington who helped to ease and pave the way for the basis of what we understand the United States to be now, through the establishment of how the government of the newly reformed country would conduct themselves back then.

Perhaps anecdotally, there were many times throughout the four months of the convention that many of the individuals in attendance questioned the integrity of the convention, in addition to whether or not it would be able to achieve what they had set out to do. Whether it was purposeful to show leadership, or merely a coincidence, throughout the months of the convention George Washington sat in a chair that had a sun painted on the back of it. After the convention, Benjamin Franklin would be noted as saying that he was never sure whether that sun was the symbol of a new time to come or was a symbol of the fact that their victory over the British was in vain. Yet as the convention was concluding, Franklin stated that the sun was rising on a new era of the United States. In other words, George Washington allowed the sun to rise on a newly established country.

Leaving the Presidential Role

Perhaps the most notable of all of Washington's achievements and moments in his presidency is how he left the position. As mentioned earlier, he refused to run for a third election for president for a variety of reasons. The first of which is that he wanted to return to his farm and family, however, the second of which, is that he wanted to set a precedent as setting the United States up as being different from the country from which they just won their independence. As a part of his voluntary exit from the presidential position, Washington sent and published A farewell address to his country through the *American Daily Advertiser* on September 19th, 1796. Within this farewell address, Washington presented himself once more as a symbol of integrity, honesty, and pure image of the ideal president.

First, he admitted to many of his downfalls and weaknesses, and asked for forgiveness from the American people. He made sure to mention that any faults, whether they be true failures or simply viewed as faults based on the opinion of the people, were made accidentally and not with any intention of harming the country. Moreover, he made sure to mention that he tried his best over his eight years of being the president, to not govern with his own biased intentions, rather the intention of the majority of the people that had elected him president twice. He made mention of the fact that he had been a humble boy with a privileged upbringing that allowed him to develop the values that he hoped he had embodied while being president.

In addition to asking for forgiveness from the American people, he also gave some words of warning to the United States population and to those political figures that would follow and succeed him. First, he warned about leaning too much on Foreign Affairs and developing long-lasting and long-term alliances between countries from other parts of the world. Washington bore witness to the fact that the events of the world changed so rapidly throughout his years, both while being president and beforehand. For this reason, he thought it wise to not form long-lasting alliances with other countries, so as to not be put in a position to make difficult decisions where the choice is between keeping the integrity of your own country or upholding your end of an agreement.

Another warning Washington made in his farewell address to the American public and political system was that he warned against creating and dividing different political parties. If political parties were to become the basis upon which elections are decided, Washington hypothesized that the candidates would no longer be seen as individuals but rather simply representative of a larger whole. As such, the voting population may become confused about who to vote for. After all they may like a candidate, however, dislike the party which they represent. Moreover, Washington predicted that the creation of different political parties will breed a sense of resentment within the United States government and would create roaring and combative political policies which do not necessarily have the good of the American public in mind, but rather, embody the biased intentions of the party.

Of course, as we have seen, the following presidents of the United States and participating members of the United States political system, have not necessarily heeded the warnings of George Washington in his farewell address. After all, how many disagreements, to put it lightly, have erupted from a difference in political opinion? Furthermore, how many individuals who claim to be loyal to their party are ostracized for simply voicing an opinion that's different from their party's tagline? Alternatively, how many future presidents felt the pressure of entering certain wars, simply due to alliances formed with other countries all over the world?

Perhaps at the time, the voluntary exit of George Washington in addition to the contents of his farewell address weren't necessarily groundbreaking. At the time, every move Washington made was the first of its kind. However, in hindsight and when we compare the United States of America now, and to what George Washington had warned against, it is interesting to note the glaring differences.

Presidential Legacy

Again, while many of his accomplishments and the memorable historical moments that happened during his tenure as leader of the United States, are highly linked to the fact that he was the first in the position—as many of them would have perhaps not have happened if it had been otherwise—many of his achievements in the political arena are notable enough to stand on their own as impressive. Two of the most memorable and influential of which are his influence on the creation of the Constitution of the United States, and the manner in which he left the presidential office yet maintained his integrity throughout his presidential run.

Humorously, two of the most influential moments within the presidency of George Washington did not actually happen within his eight-year tenure of the position. For instance, the creation of the American Constitution happened two full years before Washington was elected as the first president. Similarly, his monumental manner of exiting office happened at the end, and arguably after his tenure as president. These two impressive accolades of George Washington go to show that the reputation and legacy of one man does not necessarily have to be solely attached to what he is most known for.

* * *

"In politics as in philosophy, my tenets are few and simple. The leading one of which, and indeed that which embraces most others, is to be honest and just ourselves and to exact it from others, meddling as little as possible in their affairs where our own are not involved. If this maxim was generally adopted, wars would cease and our swords would soon be converted into reap hooks and our harvests be more peaceful, abundant, and happy." —George Washington

Chapter Five: Beyond the Politics

"Be courteous to all, but intimate with few, and let those few be well tried before you give them your confidence. True friendship is a plant of slow growth, and must undergo and withstand the shocks of adversity before it is entitled to appellation." —George Washington

When we think of the American presidents of the past, it is rare that we think of anything beyond their role and influence as political figures. In fact, to some, that is all that matters when it comes to those in any position of power, especially the president of the United States. For some presidents, their political life is all that matters, as their drive and goal to become the leader of the United States was the key motivator.

However, when we are examining the life and times of the first president of the United States, George Washington, his life outside of and beyond politics is important and worthy of note as it was his totality of achievements and virtues that he developed through his life that made him become the first leader of this free world.

Marriage to Martha

Perhaps one of the most monumental events in George Washington's life that had nothing to do with politics is his marriage to Martha Washington. Born Martha Dandridge, Washington's wife was a widow of Daniel Parke Custis, with whom she had four kids. Unfortunately, not only had she lost her husband before meeting George Washington; she had also lost two of her four children before her first husband passed. Martha, coming from a family that was considerably wealthy and well off during this time, entered the marriage with much more than just her two living children. Specifically, she came with a great many slaves to her name, in addition to a 1500-acre plot of land. This made George Washington the owner of not only the vast plantation of Mount Vernon but also Martha's land and plantation as well: two properties that Washington would split his time between and devote many hours of work as farmer and land developer, maintaining both properties and yields of crop.

For many, the marriage between Martha Dandridge, now Martha Washington, and George Washington was not a marriage that was out of the romantic or intimate kind of love. Rather, it was considered a marriage that was out of platonic, familial, and respectful love. No matter, it had proved itself to be a happy, satisfying, and all-around successful marriage for the two individuals, as both supported each other through many hardships: both personal and political.

Martha was not schooled in the formal or higher levels of education. In fact, Martha was so *uneducated* that George, at times, needed to help her with her correspondence as she was unable to read and write to the level of some of her compatriots and friends. Of course, just because Martha was uneducated, it did not mean that she lacked any sort of knowledge, nor did it mean that she was less of a woman or provider for her home. Instead, Martha Washington proved to be quite the homemaker, mother, support system, and host for her husband and family both through his political tenure and the years that bookended the presidency. This is because while she missed out on a formal education, she was schooled in the ways of being a good wife, being polite and cordial, and in the ways of conducting oneself appropriately. Characteristics that George Washington himself valued, appreciated, and overall adored of his wife.

His adoration of his wife extended to her two living children whom she brought into the new family. Washington's two stepchildren, John and Martha, were the ages of six and four respectively when their mother's marriage resulted in Washington being their stepfather. They accepted him in his new role as he accepted them as if they were his own offspring. While stories of the closeness of these individuals are few in the history books, there is a noticeable lack of any conflict between John and Martha and their stepfather, George Washington; thereby leading to the safe assumption that the three of them were rather close and their relationship was tension free.

In fact, one story of Washington's past that alludes to the closeness and admiration he had for Martha and her two children was how he acted and responded to the deaths of both John and Martha. Martha passed first at the age of 17 just before the Revolutionary War officially began. Indeed, she would never see or experience just how important her stepfather would become to other individuals. John, on the other hand, passed close to the end of the Revolutionary War. While Martha left behind no children, John left four children and a widowed wife after his passing. As there was much turmoil among the American colonies at this time, John's widow decided that her two youngest would be sent to be adopted and raised by their grandparents: George and Martha Washington. When the Revolutionary War ended, and George Washington returned home he was greeted with the opportunity to be with and raise a new family. While never having any biological children of his own, he greatly accepted his grandchildren as being his own children. However, with the newly founded country begging for a leader, specifically for George Washington to lead, Washington had no choice but to leave his familial duties once more to help run the country.

Of course, even while running the country he never forgot his love of farm life and of raising his family on the plantations. For this reason, he tried to retire after his first term in order to return to Mount Vernon and his other plantations to live out his days. Of course, again as history has told us, Washington was asked to serve once more. After his second term, Washington put his foot down on the request to run for president a third time and lived out his dream of officially and finally being able to be the family man he had always wanted to be.

Martha was a support system for him that allowed him to be impressively chosen three times to run the United States. Furthermore, it was his marriage to Martha Washington and his adoration for the family and home she had built for him that continuously reminded him of the values and virtues that a man should have in any role that he plays. While some will have different opinions of the type of military general and President Washington was, you will be hard-pressed to find anyone who disagreed with the fact that he was a virtuous man who valued hard work and honesty. His home life, culminating in his marriage to Martha, is one of those life aspects that played a large hand in maintaining his strong character.

Slave Owning

Another notable aspect to George Washington that isn't necessarily tied to his political life or military experiences is his opinions of slave owning. Having been around different plantations and compounds for the majority of his life, in addition to his wife bringing many slaves into their marriage, Washington was no stranger to the idea. In fact, Washington had been surrounded by slaves for so much of his life that the total number of slaves that he owned over time, or at one specific time is unknown as there were so many. Even the number of slaves that Martha brought into the marriage from her own family is unknown as the number was large in itself.

That being said, while he largely never questioned the role of the slaves on his plantations, he never necessarily felt comfortable with the idea and some of the practices surrounding slave owning. For example, he was always strongly against the trading and selling of slaves, whether it be between friends, or two different colonies, or countries in the world. Therefore, by not necessarily feeling comfortable with the idea of enslavement, George Washington, once officially owning his own slaves, treated them more as employees than enslaved individuals. It is said that the Washingtons had an exceptional level of care for the slaves that lived and worked on their plantations. The Washingtons would provide their slaves with more clothes than a conventional owner would; they would have the clothes of the slaves mended and cleaned regularly, which was more than what was expected at the time; the slaves were even given replacement clothes on a regular basis so as to not wear clothes that were torn and tattered too much. He gave them what he, and many others, considered to be a more than fair amount of food. He even organized annual doctor visits for every slave on any one of his plantations and compounds; this was in addition to a select few follow-up visits for any slave who had a severe illness or ailment.

As a result, there were very few slaves owned by the Washingtons that ran away or who resisted their employer. While their lives may not have been fair, they were treated better than many other slaves at the time. Over time, when the attitude towards slavery shifted, the Washingtons followed suit and freed many of their slaves; however, the majority of that was of course after Washington's death.

The Death of George Washington

One of the last moments in Washington's life that had no ties to his presidential reign is, unfortunately, his death. As Washington appreciated hard work, physical labor, and ensuring that his properties were well maintained, Washington could be found many times during his post-presidential years working himself all over the plantations and compounds. Some may argue that such a man of his age may have been working himself too hard and therefore lowered his immune system and ability to fight common ailments and simple infections. This has been hypothesized to be one of the influences and reasons for his death.

On the 12th of December in 1799, Washington spent the day riding around his plantation, in weather that was less than ideal. Consequently, Washington woke up with a bad cold. After fighting the cold for two days, it was decided and found that he had a throat infection. Not being able to fight off the throat infection on his own, in addition to his doctors not knowing how to treat a throat infection of this kind, Washington died on December 14th, 1799.

Near the last hours of Washington's life, he was recorded as saying that he could feel himself going and that the doctors should let him be at peace. Unable to refute and heal him even if they tried, the doctors allowed Washington to pass peacefully in his bed while being surrounded by his loving wife and grandchildren.

The death of George Washington sent ripples of tragedy throughout many areas of the world. For months, different states all around the newly independent country mourned the death of their first president. In other parts of the world, Napoleon declared a 10-day mourning period in order to give the first president of the United States the reverence and respect he deserved. Additionally, there was mourning in England as well, the very country from which the United States won their independence. It is said that the British Royal Navy flew their flags at half-mast for many days upon hearing of the passing of George Washington.

The kind of dignity Washington had on his deathbed, followed by the immense amount of respect leaders from all over the world had for this great man, truly proves and exemplifies the love and respect many had for the very first president of the United States.

While there are many monumental moments in George Washington's Political life and presidency that make him such a notable character in American history, it is his accomplishments and life beyond politics that really make up the legacy that he left behind.

* * *

"I hope I shall possess firmness and virtue enough to maintain what I consider the most enviable of all titles, the character of an honest man." —George Washington

Chapter Six: The Legacy of George Washington

"If freedom of speech is taken away, then dumb and silent we may be led, like sheep to the slaughter." —*George Washington*

Definitionally speaking, a legacy refers to those physical objects and things that are left behind and passed on, in and through someone's will. Usually, these items are based on some sort of monetary or property value. However, when it comes to the legacy of a notable person in history, like for example the first president of the United States, it involves so much more. Their legacy includes not only what they left behind physically and as possessions, but it also refers to who they left behind, such as friends and family. In addition, the lessons, ideas, inspiration, and overall reputation and mark they left on those people that followed them are paramount. As the first president of the United States, the legacy of George Washington is an interesting and notable one.

While many at the time and in our modern day were unsure whether or not Washington was perhaps the perfect president, it is perhaps unanimously agreed that he was the perfect ideal of a president, simply based on the fact that he embodied the character, dignity, and humility required in order to run a country. It is this character of being that is the legacy of George Washington.

As part of his eulogy, Henry Lee, a military Captain who worked alongside Washington during and before the Revolutionary war said:

[George Washington was] "First in war, first in peace, and first in the hearts of his countrymen, he was second to none in humble and enduring scenes of private life. Pious, just, humane, temperate, and sincere; uniform, dignified, and commanding; his example was as edifying to all around him as were the effects of that example lasting... Such was the man for whom our nation mourns" —Captain Henry Lee

This opinion was held by many who surrounded and knew Washington well during his lifetime. From his childhood to the day of his death, Washington was known to be a courageous young man who never outwardly backed down from a challenge. He had leadership skills that, while different from those classic forms and figures of leadership at that time, proved to be exemplary and effective. Many believe that his leadership skills were so effective due to the fact that he practiced a humble and honest form of confidence; one that individuals related to and admired.

Of course, this opinion of the character and personhood of George Washington was not unfounded. The traits that were seen in Washington were exemplified in his political actions and beliefs, which further justified the high regard given to the first president of the United States. He exemplified humility as a leader and was not afraid to ask for aid and advice when he felt as though he needed it. Furthermore, he is said to have set the stage of expectation for how all future presidents of the United States should conduct themselves: as honest men who, while keeping in mind their own intentions and bias for the country, are looking to make compromises for the greater good and betterment of their people of the United States.

Monuments and In Memorandum

To ensure that the legacy of George Washington stays in the minds of every citizen of the United States, there have been many monuments and memorial tributes made to George Washington, some of which are well-known to the American public, while others are perhaps unfamiliar.

Some of the more obvious tributes are the face of Washington appearing on the $1 coin and Bill, and on every quarter. Washington has also appeared on the United States postage stamp countless times. Of course, in addition to the image of Washington appearing all over the United States, there are larger monuments that have been erected and built in the image and respect of the first president. For example, on the 21st of February 1885, the Washington Monument was finally and officially finished and posthumously given to George Washington. The idea to create a Washington Monument was agreed upon moments after Washington left the presidency, but due to a lack of funds and other affecting factors, it was not finished until 1885. To this day the Washington Monument stands at 600 feet tall as a sort of Egyptian obelisk dedicated to George Washington.

Another well-known nod to Washington is of course Mount Rushmore. In 1941, the stone monument with the faces of four of the arguably most influential United States presidents, was created and finished. Today, George Washington rests on Mount Rushmore alongside President Thomas Jefferson, President Theodore Roosevelt, and President Abraham Lincoln.

Of course, the Monuments and dedications do not stop there. The name of George Washington has been used many times all over the United States and the world. George Washington is the only president of the United States to have a state named after him, while in addition to this state nomenclature, his name was also used for the nation's capital, Washington DC. Furthermore, multiple post-secondary institutions have used the Washington name within theirs.

Lastly, Washington remains to be in the top-20 most popular street names within the United States of America.

The variety of these monuments and tributes to the first president of the United States goes to show that although the controversy of whether or not Washington in fact did enough during his tenure as president, it is his character and personhood that has had a lasting effect over not only the population of the United States but also of the world.

Ultimately, the legacy that George Washington has left behind for the American people is that character is an important part of the person you are in addition to the person you've become. If Washington had not presented himself in such a way as being dignified, respectful, and as a man who was not willing to forego or abandon his virtues, then he perhaps would not have made it as far as he had in his personal and political endeavors. Many history books discuss his political compatriots claiming that he was not necessarily the greatest military commander, nor did he have a stronghold in his understanding of politics; weaknesses that Washington himself admitted to having. However, it is the fact that Washington was not too proud to admit to these weaknesses but was confident enough to bring the American Colonies together as one unified and free democratic country that pushed him to be an influential figure and president. In other words, the population of the United States saw George Washington as someone they cannot only relate to, but someone they could trust with their country and livelihoods.

This legacy of George Washington has turned into an ideal and expectation that is placed upon many political figures that have succeeded him; unfortunately, it is an idea and expectation that is often failed and abandoned.

* * *

"But lest some unlucky event should happen unfavorable to my reputation, I beg it may be remembered by every gentleman in the room that I this day declare with the utmost sincerity, I do not think myself equal to the command I am honored with." —
George Washington

Final Words

"The turning points of lives are not the great moments. The real crises are often concealed in occurrences so trivial in appearance that they pass unobserved." —George Washington

As a young man, George Washington most likely did not grow up yearning or dreaming of being the president of the United States, mostly because the job had yet to be created. Similarly, he most likely did not think he would be in such a position of power to be one of the Founding Fathers of a nation. Instead, although he had shown incredible leadership skills throughout his life, every event in Washington's life leading up to his presidency showed that he simply wanted to live on his plantation, cultivate his land, and raise his family. However, as the passage of time has shown us, even the best-laid plans change. It goes to show that even when the United States was being formed, the patriotism towards the new country was as strong as it could have been. After all, agreeing to serve as the leader of a new country, twice for that matter, out of a sense of duty rather than a sense of desire, is perhaps the largest act of patriotism there is.

Unfortunately for George Washington, it is still contested to this day whether or not he did enough as the first president of the United States. That is, taking up the role of the first presidency, against his desire to do so, so that the people of the United States would have a determined leader, was not enough. Some individuals claim that he should have stayed for at least one more term to ensure that the idea of presidency he had set were being upheld, rather than simply leaving politics and living out his days at Mount Vernon. Others claim that while two terms was more than enough, he should have done more within his two terms to solidify certain presidential procedures and party etiquette rather than simply attempting to organize the country. For example, he could have set laws in place to ensure that a multi-party country and relationships to become allies with other countries overseas were not developed; this is of course in contrast to simply warning about the dangers of these two political aspects.

However, these critiques of the Washington presidency are rather small when compared to perhaps the largest criticism of the Washington presidency. Namely that it was the most opportune time to abolish slavery in the new country: something that wasn't abolished until the 16th president of the United States, Abraham Lincoln. Interestingly, abolishing slavery was on the agenda at one point during this time, and Washington did contemplate it. However, it was the members of his cabinet and other political figures that thought abolishing slavery while trying to establish a new nation was too much for the population of the United States. Therefore, the idea was abandoned for many years.

Even with this criticism, it is hard to ignore that the presidency of George Washington was monumental in its own right—it and he were the first of their kind. Everything he did while performing the role of president was new and unique. Of course, the negative view of Washington's presidential run is an opinion that many have had for a number of past presidents. This is unfortunate because with Washington, as well as with many of the past presidents, they are largely judged on what they have done and accomplished through the standards of our modern era. Whether this is a fair standard and lens through which to examine life, for the presidency of Washington, one thing is for certain; George Washington, the first president of the United States, Founding Father, Commander of the Continental Army, was a man full of charm, courage, and leadership. After all, who else would be brave enough to be the first leader of a newly freed nation?

* * *

"Where are our Men of abilities? Why do they not come forth to save their Country?" —George Washington

George Washington Timeline of Notable Life Events

- **1732**

  - On the 22nd of February 1732, Mary Bell Washington gives birth to her first child and son, George Washington, with her husband Augustine Washington.

- **1743**

  - At the age of only 11, Augustine Washington, George's father passed away, leaving his inheritance and plantations to his family. George is tasked with caring for his mother and siblings while finishing school.

- **1746**

  - It is said that in the year 1746, George Washington read the book *The Rules of Civility*, a book about manners and proper protocol. The contents of which dictated and influenced the type of man he grew up to be.

- **1751**

  - At the age of nineteen, Washington took a trip to the Bahamas, accompanied by his older, half-brother, Lawrence. According to some, it was on this trip that Washington contracted and survived smallpox.

- **1753**

  - On the 31st of October in 1753, after already being in battle, Washington officially joined the military.

- **1758**

  - On the 24th of July, Washington officially entered the political arena. He was elected to be the representative of Frederick County as a part of Virginia's House of Burgesses Government.

- **1759**

  - George Washington married Martha Custis on the 6th of January. She brought two children into this marriage with George from a previous one where her husband had died.

- **1761**

  - Washington became the official owner of Mount Vernon; a property that will forever be known and attributed to the first president of the United States of America.

- **1766**

  - Even though it was a family crop, in the mid 1700s George Washington decided to stop growing Tobacco on his land and opted to grow wheat products instead.

- **1775**

  - On June 15th, 1775, Washington was named Commander in Chief of the army throughout the American Revolution.

- **1776**

  - On December 25th, Washington led a secret mission across the Delaware River. It was a move and battle that led to the victory of the Americans during the revolution and was a large influence on Washington becoming the leader of the new nation.

- **1789**

  - On April 30th, 1789, George Washington was made the first president of the United States. He was inaugurated in New York City; the first capital of the country.

- **1791**

  - As part of his presidency, Washington decides to travel around the newly formed and independent nation to meet all those who are now part of his country.

- **1792**

  - Again, George Washington was chosen and made to be the president of the United States. This inauguration was in Philadelphia, the new capital of the United States.

- **1797**

  - George Washington decides to not run for president, or any political office, after being in the position himself for eight years. This is despite being essentially offered the position for the third time. Therefore, it is assumed that if he had run for president for a third term, he would have won.

- **1799**

  - On December the 14th of 1799, George Washington passed away at the age of 67. He was buried in his homestead at Mount Vernon. It was a death that shook the still newly formed nation for several months and years to follow.

References

Liles, M. (2021, February 1). *Get Ready for Presidents Day With 125 Quotes From George Washington*. Parade. https://parade.com/989259/marynliles/george-washington-quotes/